AF323762

Abigail Adams
Alex Chaves

Penny-Ante Editions
Success and Failure Series
Catalogue No. PA-022
978-0-9785564-6-4

Abigail Adams

Abigail Adams
Table of Contents

Por

Willa

Here's the thing about us:
we'll meet after
    all this shit settles
everyone is a minefield, but you I trust

Women are like lighthouses,
few exist anymore
women don't have to be women anymore
some still want to

I don't understand why you don't run
around screaming in a gravel parking lot
like a banshee with your tits hanging out
cause that's all I'd want to do
if I had
    your tits

A love
that even
time-
would stand
still
for

I say the serenity prayer
feeling wrong
soaked, desperate, and penniless
all the inconsequential
longings of lovers
come and gone

I rub a coin and think of the
curve of your jaw
the stump of my pride
Early in the morning
I trip and am clumsy
it takes so many
deep breaths to be
refined

Is your beauty cumulative?
Did it arrive suddenly
missing the point
being at a loss for words
getting déjà vu
and just chilling

You peer around the room
I'm staring at you
The back of your arms are nice you
   stand erect
I diffuse into
a million ideas of you

Something about you is
all-American
It's erotic and hygenic
You smell like soap and keep
   your things in order

Ignoring your call
Heavily
I continue on my endless errands
    this is my life

I'm going to send an email
so large and hefty

I want to know the security code
to your house

I.D.

I.D.

All these compensations and platitudes
breeze in and out of me what can I say.
Getting caught up in word choice. I had
a thought yesterday that I prefer to know
women because they are wiser because
their bodies are attached to time and nature
in a way that makes them understand the
urgency and fleeting quality of life.

I can smile. I can be evocative. I can
sound sure and speculative
simultaneously.

Parsing out distinction is just like this
full-time job.

"Growing up I was constantly in a state of fear. My birth parents put me up for adoption when I was born. A happy healthy adoptive family was a dream that never came true. Bouncing in and out of foster care was the reality of my life. At 8 years old, I was finally adopted. You might want to even say bought as a slave. It all was too good to be true. I was selected and moved to upstate New York. The beauty of the suburbs was something I had never experienced or witnessed. What my father did to me will haunt me forever. My relationships, work, and happiness is dwindled down to feeling numb."

JACK CHAVES 2014

Just beside me, here lay a homely woman
down beside me she groove gnarly

underneath the brambles
there a gull's nest
step by step we're getting to know
    each other

Life is slapping me around, and I'm getting
    slap happy
Here's a penchant I keep close

*"Them that's got shall get, them
that's not shall lose, so the Bible said,
and it still is news . . . "*

I couldn't find a subject about you, or a
purpose to want you – being charmed is
so different than being taught. I keep
thinking that life is a school and God is

a teacher. I keep wondering where to keep
the battered people.

How much and if life is about
healing?

Aging
worked on him like a sauna
after many a summer

Julianne

You know how when something happens to
you, you see it everywhere?

We're driving down the Bowery and there's
this guy in a banana costume, and it's hot,
so hot – the kids are very sympathetic to
people in costumes, what I tend to look
for in my work is what makes us alike, not
what makes us different,
I didn't know L.A. existed, I was
    so incredibly naïve
I literally got off the bus in my dress with a
suitcase in hand.

There is duality in what you do,
your face changes,
you look like one thing and then you smile
and you look like something else

when you share a sensibility
    with someone,
If you start to confuse your life with things
that are ephemeral, it will kill you.

I had a fever dream: we were speeding
through the amazon on the way to our
school at the tip of Chile. I was traveling
with two redheads, they were like me,
but a little more deformed. There was
a snowstorm in the forecast, and I was
scared to drive down there. I kept feeling
this fear of snow, the intense feeling of
rain, and I was sweating the bed.

What am I afraid of?

CRACKALACK

I need a severance package for my
panic attack –

If I stay
    dancing
hopped up like I'm on crackalack.

My OWN LOVE SONG

Drop by my place unexpectedly
I live on a street corner
My albatross

Behind my back
And over my shoulder
Blood from a stone

Talking to people exasperates my patience
When I see something beautiful
    it shuts me up

I want to give you permission
    yet
there's an elephant in the room

I want to ascribe my anxiety to you
The poison between my fingers
A rupture that did not cease
A well so deep and red

The jugs you made
A self-help book we're too proud to read

Men who are

VIRTUOUS

SIMPLE

CLEAN

LIGHT

KIND

for

you

I'd
explore the entire surface of your body
for articles of dismay and quiet perfection,
watch you from afar,
apply sunscreen dutifully.

I know I need the entire day to myself.

I'm always looking for a pendant of you;
I want a badge.

Nut Cracker

I remember seeing Jack in the Nutcracker.
He played Fritz. The rat kings and the
sugar plums. Two children amongst the
hallucinations of a Christmas spell.
Their movements were strict, animated
and artificial. All of the fuss and ridicu-
lousness of ballet. All the asses in colored
tights. Tchaikovsky is transportive and
mystical. Maybe it wasn't all bullshit,
maybe God is a yellow light. Fantasia might
not be different from God – believing in
beauty and scouring for it. Seeing
phantoms and a parade of traditions
resonating in different parts of my psyche.
The poinsettias and handcrafted ornaments
made by children in Sunday schools.
How putting glitter to tinfoil might channel
Jesus or some shit.

Our dreams stand so close to the drudgery
of the everyday. How many ways there
are to depict an angel. I got stoned and
saw the fabric flowers not as fake, but as
permanent and needing to be watched
and clarifying an ideal form. I understand
why you'd want to grow a garden, or order
fresh flowers – their humanity. But still,
I get mixed up between the soul of a
material and the shape of its body. The
ringing of the bells, the delicate mastery
of the orchestra coaxed the body into
something wetter. Feeling dewey and
fluid (peeing, drooling, sweating, crying).
Fantasy was not a retreat nor an incident.
It's careful construction came slowly
and totally. You might be a wood nymph
or a pinecone, might be washed over,
your cock might disagree with you.
An unexpected erection.

Your face and entire body could wield to
a vast glittering temple, a vision cast on
you by the simple turning of a hip, hint of
a smile.

Fashion

That sounds wonderful but I'm having
emotional moments in the studio and
digesting misgivings of last night and
drinking coffee. I'll think I'll drink a gallon
of sparkling water today.

I am up to no good at this gay tennis
tournament cocktail hour.

Pilgrim, cowboy, gnome.
I'm always talking all this trash. Like
    I'll be Elizabeth Murray
or Joan Mitchell. Is that misogynist?

upper lip
  holocaust scholar
    acid trip
      long hair
        race car driver . . .

I've always thought I would fall for
someone foreign, the familiar is so
distasteful in romance. I was born with an
adventurous heart and I don't apologize.
Another thing I advocated in the past: to
dream of decency and verisimilitude, of
gall and cruelty. I want a soft relationship
with someone who understands cruelty.
A middle-aged man told me I had knowing
eyes. An irritable disposition. I emit bitch
because life is richer with scorn.

Why is everyone getting away with
everything? Why do we have to celebrate
our perversities tonight, I want to regress
on top of you, get to know your bod. Buying
home goods is a good solution to feeling
out of control. As is cleaning. Feng shui is
real, aromatherapy is real, sun gazing is
real, going for walks – also real.

What's the point of writing a book you
don't make any money and it's so fucking
hard. He talks to me like I need to be pet,
wants to make a wretch out of me and
I let him because I'm complacent. Empty
and inscrutable. Not sure how I walked
into being the guidance counselor but here
I am. Leading an exemplary life is unat-
tainable due to the possibility of privacy.
People want things from you. I like woeful
songs about success like Joni Mitchell's
"For Free". My little idea to organize a
show called, *Latina Painting Now*.

I want to look ancient. It takes so much
manipulation to keep the body under
control. I like to tell people that I live
in squalor, but I'm always negotiating how
bad my taste really is. How rough my life
really is or was or will be. Why am I
always strategizing? Should I tell him that
I dreamed of him all last night and it felt
turbulent and sea-sick. I have a tendency
towards quickly forgotten fever dreams.
It's funny when people complain about art
being so sexless, unerotic these days. If
your poetry isn't confessional, honestly
why bother?

1969

Fuck my sad healthy pasta
but it was actually good

I like the obvious
physical comedy
playful wit

I'm not fucking anne carson

Why would you want to fucking get to
    know me?
I can't hang out with him
But I'm going to
Maybe I'll make him pose for me
I guess I could use him for his looks

When I think about having sex with women
I imagine Tuscany
fresh basil and tomatoes
a sundress
I associate "women" with Italy I guess

Everybody plays the fool
I like things that are stupid and true

Having sex I just feel like I'm tripping out
I'm learning to stand still
I'm in a period of radical self-discovery

Love Song II

I was trying to get on your wavelength
If we could be on the same plane
Then maybe

But no
    no
I found you; I dump seeds in faces to
give them ideas

Beauty is a liar
Humility is a liar

I wake up seering and cloudy
I don't exactly wish you well
Stay away from me until I want you there
You're just an actor, a prop, a symbol
And I am the sea.

People

Waiting for the truth is like missing the bus

An unsquashable beauty routine but
your face doesn't hide the places
    you've been

I walk into the bar like a prince and
    no one is amused
I wouldn't blame you for aversion to my
tartness

People who don't realize their
personalities are experiences in the world
People without style
People with bad taste

They're out there

a date with Elena

In the garden
of the retreat center
on Ellis Island
during the driest spring on record
I will writhe down
my salt scrubbed bodice
encrusted with white shells
atop the algaed, storied boulders and
shake it steady.

HATE POEM

I do not remember every face of every
man
    who put me here

I got no love
I hate to work
I hate to suffer
I hate to be a turning part of a machine
I hate to be a server

I hope you saunter tonight
I hope there's a garland around your ankle

I'm always smoking
He has a dignified way of standing that
    makes me sick

How dare you
Honestly how dare you

What are you?

    (a rich, sensuous life robust with
    exploration, consideration, and beauty
    in all respects)

That's more than most people have
yet so much more despicable

the Philosopher's Stone

My legacy,
how will you remember me?
I have to confront what you look like
first thing in the morning
I am afraid this parking structure might
    fall on me.
I work hard for you.
I want to be guided, to have a life with
    meaning I can point towards.
Anyone can write and so I will too.
The most important thing I try to get
across is that whatever I am,
whatever I look like,
whatever I'm doing – it's urgent.

I can't get over this problem I have.

Oppositions are
pedestrian,
ordinary.

To be clear, I am not a philosopher.
I'm trying to talk about earthly wisdom
    behind flashy things.
There's always something older.
I don't want to get caught up in the
    devastated trenches of history.
I want to start over.
I long for a world with less
injustice, carelessness, brutality, and
    simplicity.

I want to give you the poetry of our racist
fathers.

My Afflicted Face

My afflicted face.
What was it you told me about my
    astrological chart?
I was amongst the outer waves of the
tropic of cancer
was born on a hot bloody
full moon in fall 1744

I get morose – it comes easily, naturally.
I dangle a potpourri of secrecy and danger
My expectations are endless
How is anyone worth it?
I have to be wooed into loving you

It's not that I think I'm ugly or totally
horrific to witness,
but it's hard to just be the one thing

When you said I was your favorite artist
were you being facetious?

How much space do you take up?
I don't understand people who don't need
their lives to be grand.

I'm fine with being wrong.

I step over all the clutter into the bathroom
and gaze longingly at
my afflicted face.

Without You

Without you I'm something else
    in the street.
Your staunch posture
the way you stood before me unashamed

w/o you:
    A fierce desire to be recognized.
    Scary to look at.

I won't end.
I repeat, rewind the tape
back to the part –
I was glad to have met you
had time to kill
didn't think of money.

How I did awake,
muddled and fragrant
with the caress of a
steam of a man I could
not love, nay hardly
admire. None of them
shine like the man I
dreamed of last night
who kept me fast asleep
whilst an electrical fire
sparked next door.

telling you my shit

I resent my powerlessness today.
My routine is inextinguishable.
Let's talk about the difficulties of traveling;
not knowing where to
    shit, sleep, eat, or drink.
It's dangerous to conflate your desires
with those of your company.

This isn't somewhere nice.
I want to put my body in contact with the
    ground,
I don't mind it here.
I start telling you my shit.
Do you think about everything you say as
potential evidence in your persecution?

Being base embarrasses me,
the things I fixate on humiliate me,
I wonder if I'm using my time right or
if I'm living fully enough.
My attachments exhaust and degrade me.

I wake up late.
I avoid participation in suffering.
I think they'll hire me for my arts.
We are not the dignity girls.

Is there a trivial life?

Dating

I'm not ready to see you
I spend days getting ready

Considering calling you interests me
    enough to squash efforts
spending time with anyone else
I want to be hearty and a flirt
I'm distant and aloof in substitute
Don't play your magic on me
Don't you do your voodoo on me boy

Did I take advantage of you
The lack of availability of anything decent
    to eat in this neighborhood
I make out with boys like we're girls
    or French
I don't give a shit about
owing anything to men

Stop trying to decide what you are
Write it down before you forget it
It's medicinal what we do now

Gwyneth

She came barrelling into the world,
I knew she'd be a force of nature.
She didn't invent a new way to be bad,
she was bad in the way you were supposed
to be bad.

You got a nice face you should let the boys
see it

   — it ain't my face the boys want to see

My mouth is worn down
The grimy film on everything I say
Having conversations
I'm negotiating distance
I can't locate my honesty

Women on couches having conversations
over a cup of tea
I have a shame complex
I can't believe it

Not having my time be mine
  again is such a shock.

Working scares me so much
It makes me tremble and defiant
I can't be on someone else's watch
Can't be in someone else's company
Only in privacy do I become myself

Flower St.

Rabid in the street downtown
There are people here I want euthanized
I'm an unshaven rat
They made this city so ugly

Someone is yelling at me
I'm trying to take my time
I've felt sexy in this tacky cafe
I don't know how we got here
    but we're staying

Do you always remember your first love?
Writing without looking
I do it all without paying any attention to it
it's so charming

How many mentally ill people
   have you had sex with?
Move to the country with me
I wanna publish it
I wanna move to the next phase of my life

My own Love Song

III

At the point where our glances
just failed to meet,
I created a series of complaints
Which I filed in my image of you
The volume of your voice,
I wanted to call you out. But I couldn't until
after the fact,
I harass you until you are harassed.

I liked her unfinished poems
I thought of the person she might become
She gathered maxims and resolutions
The mouse that scurries around a
conversation

The trails in your apartment
My disruption
Waking up early

What am I besides your corruption?

Better yet
Let's stand here and leaf through our
    correspondence
Let's discover a family
        between us.
Isn't it obvious,
there's more here to uncover?
I thought my desperation was clear.

Baby

father

I'm in a meeting. There are carpeted floors and familiar faces, but one man in the group does not belong. The day feels mundane; suddenly we are stuck in the room. The lock is broken and we have to wait for a locksmith to let us out. Everyone is exasperated and takes out their cell phones to call or text their friends and family members to tell them that they are locked in this room for an unknown amount of time. The man in the room who does not belong is some sort of social invalid, perhaps a homeless man or autistic. His presence has the general sense of being unwelcome, he looks unshowered and there is a group discomfort directed towards him. Without warning, someone pulls out a gun. They shoot the unwanted man. I see the first bullet make its way through

his chest. The force shakes his body and blood sprays.

A sense of horror and alarm captivates the crowd and silences their conversations. The man with the gun shoots the ugly man again and again and now my vision really focuses on the body of the invalid. There is so much gore, I have never seen a body desecrated like this in real life. It feels different from depictions in film and television. The ugly man is shot in the eye and it looks like his eye explodes; part of his innards spill out. I feel sick, and I vomit after the murderer shoots the ugly man. The nausea is overwhelming. I am completely undone and servant to my environment. My surrounding antagonizes me. It looks milky on the generic red carpeting.

The next time I see the murderer he is
handcuffed to a chair. His baby is next to
him in a crib. The baby is crying. I am
surprised to discover that he has a child.
He speaks to me, "Please, my baby has
been crying all day, he needs someone
to hold him, I can't because I am hand-
cuffed." The murderer is desperate, close
to tears. He begs me to help him. He says,
"PLEASE HE NEEDS SOMEONE TO
HOLD HIM." I oblige, and recognize the
innocence of the murderer's child. I pick
up the baby out of its crib and hold him in
my arms. I then, perhaps quizzically,
decide to sit in the chair next to the
murderer with his baby. The baby starts
to settle down and his crying stops. I look
at the eyes of the murderer. They look
watery and glassy, he looks afraid. He
is trembling.

I stay there for a while next to him with his child in my hands. He starts to look at me, reaches for me. I begin to understand him, and then to covet him. I feel so deeply for him, as I could be his only advocate. I start to swell and we stay there exploring in glance for a while.

Fourth of July

Taking a break from painting who never
lets me down.
We can joke about it
but you know how
utterly ugly it feels to be alive, right?

Flip a coin
come up with a new problem
use a diversion tactic
you don't get knowledge
you don't just get it

I love the dream bed I've made for myself
I wonder if men can feel my power
a tawny rat in the bedroom
    yes
yes it is me.

What happened to the rage boy?
What happened to him?
AMERICA

Made you throw all your big words around
and seduce every cliché on top of me
I don't care I don't give a shit at all
I want it right now

Beware I am the descendant of a
thousand mad men
Going about it in the way that it's always
been done
using the tools
you have available to you

Poetry is so call and response to itself like
what even is that I love it.

I'm emerging
I'm an emerging author.

My plan is to have a wild day and then
be civil and get dressed to have drinks
There are obstacles, fatigues,
reasons to stop
you from enforcing your will
unto the world
To refuse them
is the greatest power
and longest loss
a young king will know

Rations and trepidations
for the day we all have to get through
I love you like the
romance of
what the fuck

A fresh page redeems me before I spill
all over again
all over my community

Abigail Adams
Alex Chaves

Penny-Ante Editions
Success and Failure Series
Catalogue No. PA-022
978-0-9785564-6-4

Abigail Adams is printed in conjunction with *The Amerikan Green Cross* exhibition (Night Gallery, Los Angeles) in an edition of 350.

Cover photographs & illustrations by Alex Chaves
Book design by Penny-Ante
Set in Lyon Text, Tiempos Headline & Gross
Printed in the United States of America

Penny-Ante Editions
P.O. Box 691578 Los Angeles, California 90069
United States of America
penny–ante.net